Effective Teaching

THE CORNERSTONE OF QUALITY EDUCATION

James V. Foran, Ed.D.

PARADIGM

This book is dedicated to my wife, Lise. One day our children, Rachel and Ian, will realize how lucky they have been to have her as their first master teacher.

Project Editors	Janice Johnson
	Jeffrey W. Josephson
Copyeditor	Mary C. Konstant
Proofreader	Elyse Duffy
Cover Design	Kris Nelson
Composition	James Kostello

ISBN 1-56118-101-3

Copyright © 1990 Published by EMC/Paradigm Publishing
875 Montreal Way
Saint Paul, Minnesota 55102-4245
(800)535-6865
E-mail: publish@emcp.com

Printed in the United States of America

CONTENTS

Part II: Observation of Live Instruction

James V. Foran, Vice President for Educational Affairs for the Association of Independent Colleges and Schools (AICS), provided the vision for the *Effective Teaching* project and also served as the author of this book. Dr. Foran has long had a keen interest in improving the quality of teaching at all levels of education.

Dr. Foran began his career as a classroom teacher in Prince George's County, Maryland. He was then appointed to the position of high school principal, where he served for eight years. Following his public school experience, Foran joined the Commonwealth College system, where he served as school director and later as Director of Operations and Academic Affairs. He assumed his present position with AICS in November 1987.

In both the public schools and at AICS, Dr. Foran has received recognition for outstanding achievements. He is an Honorary Lifetime Member of the Maryland Congress of Parents and Teachers. He is the recipient of the Distinguished Educator Award from the Charles F. Kettering Foundation. Prince George's County Public Schools selected him as Outstanding Educator. At its recent annual meeting, AICS presented him with the Distinguished Service Award.

Dr. Foran is the coauthor of *Quality Assurance for Private Career Schools*. Following the publication of that book, he presented a series of twelve workshops throughout the country to assist private career schools in adapting industrial quality assurance principles to education. Dr. Foran is a frequent speaker and writer on a wide variety of educational topics including leadership, outcomes assessment, classroom instruction, instructional supervision, and management for quality.

ACKNOWLEDGMENTS

On behalf of the Association of Independent Colleges and Schools, I wish to acknowledge the generous contributions of Paradigm Publishing International in the production of this faculty development package. While others have talked about wanting to improve the quality of teaching, Paradigm has delivered. Without blinking an eye about the cost of the book or accompanying video, this new company has elevated the discussion of professional growth among faculty to a new level. In the process, Paradigm Publishing International steps forward as a major player in educational publishing. For the countless students who will be the beneficiaries, I say thank you.

I also wish to acknowledge Francis G. Tracy, my seventh-grade English teacher. By the time I graduated from college, Frank had become a junior high school principal. He gave me my first job as a classroom teacher, and his subsequent impact on my career has been extraordinary. Frank is an inspiration who convinced me there is no nobler profession than teaching. He also taught me how to teach. Without Frank Tracy's influence, this book would never have been written.

Lastly, I thank the instructors who volunteered their time to appear in the video and assist with other aspects of this project.

James V. Foran

INTRODUCTION

Effective teaching! What is it? How do you know when you see it? How do you know when you are doing it? How do you know if your students are learning? What are the characteristics of an effective school? These are but a few of the many difficult questions that have plagued educators for centuries. This workbook will not provide all the answers, but it will simplify the body of knowledge that presently exists. Its major purpose is to help subject area experts become more effective classroom teachers.

While other treatments dealing with effective teaching emphasize theoretical concepts, this workbook is a practitioner's guide. Used in conjunction with the accompanying video, it will demystify and simplify an extremely complex topic — effective teaching — without diminishing the enormous challenges teachers face. Although theory is presented, the major focus is practical experience for new instructors and for those who wish to continue to grow in their profession.

No such effort could possibly replace the hours of study and real-life experience required to become a master teacher. However, a working knowledge of the basics of teaching as provided in this workbook and video will provide a firm foundation upon which you can build your skills as an effective teacher.

PERFORMANCE OUTCOMES

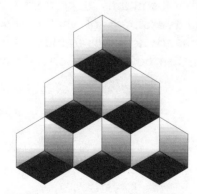

Each chapter in the workbook has practice activities that participants are expected to complete. Several major outcomes are intended for the workbook and video:

► The teacher should be able to produce a course outline indicating major course and lesson performance outcomes for students.

► The teacher should be able to prepare an effective lesson plan complete with all appropriate components.

► The teacher should be able to evaluate instructor effectiveness in a variety of lessons that use different modes of instruction.

In a companion workbook, suggestions will be provided for instructional leaders so they can evaluate the degree to which teachers have met these outcomes.

TARGET AUDIENCE

Teachers and instructional supervisors at all levels can benefit from this workbook and video. Though the materials were developed for the Association of Independent Colleges and Schools, the content is applicable to any teacher, regardless of background and experience. Our underlying assumption is that all teachers (effective or ineffective) can improve if they are committed to teaching excellence and professional growth.

USE OF WORKBOOK AND VIDEO

Participants should view the first part of the video once before reading the workbook. After the initial viewing, participants should read the workbook and stop where suggested either to do performance activities or to view the remainder of the video. Small group settings are appropriate for both viewing the video and completing workbook activities.

The terms **student/learner** and **teacher/instructor** are used interchangeably throughout the workbook. This usage is intentional: it should remove any doubt regarding the appropriate level for this material. We believe that similar elements are present in all effective instruction. Planning curriculum and performance outcomes, delivering relevant instruction, and evaluating learning may change based upon the design of the instruction and the styles of the learners and instructor, but truly effective teaching looks virtually the same at any level.

ROLE OF INSTRUCTIONAL SUPERVISOR

These materials are intended to be self-paced and self-contained. It would, however, be helpful and desirable if the instructional supervisor took a leadership role in their use. In addition to completing this workbook, the instructional supervisor should complete the companion workbook designed specifically for those charged with the responsibility of improving instruction. That workbook contains suggestions for improving supervisory skills as well as examples of what to look for in teacher responses to performance activities found in this workbook. Supervisors will also learn how to deal effectively with those responses.

PART I
WHAT IS EFFECTIVE TEACHING?

The aim of teachers and the school curricula should be to awaken, not "stock" or "train" the mind. We need to help students be aware of what they don't know that is worth knowing.

Grant Wiggins

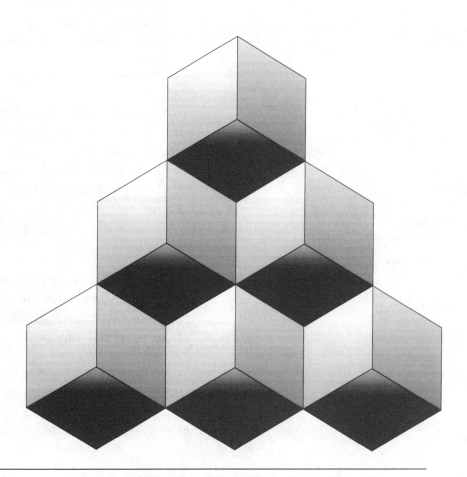

EFFECTIVE SCHOOLS

Much research exists on effective schools, but most of it is for the K-12 level. At the risk of overgeneralizing the research findings, we should be aware of characteristics of effective schools as identified in the studies. Researchers contend that these characteristics transfer to postsecondary education. You are encouraged, however, to evaluate each characteristic individually as it applies to your school.

Edmonds (1979, 1982), Miles, Farrar, and Neufeld (1983), Brookover and Lezotte (1977), and others have completed extensive studies in this area. A synthesis of the available research indicates that certain characteristics appear with regularity in effective schools:

- Clear and focused mission that serves as the cornerstone for the instructional program
- Instructional leader who has the responsibility of accomplishing the mission and who is a visible leader in the school
- High level of time on task in the classroom
- High expectations of students and staff
- Frequent monitoring of student progress
- Safe and orderly environment conducive to teaching and learning
- Parental and community involvement in the school

A quick glance at the characteristics suggests that most, if not all, are equally applicable to other sectors of education. Although wording and emphasis may change, postsecondary as well as K-12 sectors of education would be well served to strive for these characteristics in each institution.

TRADITIONAL INSTRUCTION vs. SYSTEMATIC INSTRUCTIONAL DESIGN

If we assume there are common elements that tend to identify effective schools, then similarly are there elements that identify effective classroom instruction? There are two broad categories of instructional theory: traditional instruction and systematic instructional design.

Gagne and Briggs (1979), Johnson (1989), Van Patten (1989), and others have attempted to distinguish between these two separate approaches to instruction. Simply stated, these experts tend to consider traditional instruction as content oriented. Such instruction typically includes standardized curricula, course syllabi, and course outlines. Rarely does traditional instruction deal with teaching strategies and performance outcomes, at least in authentic and measurable terms. Certainly learners are important in traditional instruction, but the focus is overwhelmingly on content and standardization of what is taught. Instructors are expected to cover that content regardless of the time available or the performance outcomes intended from the instruction.

Systematic instructional design, on the other hand, requires more thought and planning prior to the teaching/learning process. In contrast to the content orientation of traditional instruction, instructional design concerns itself with the learner. Performance outcomes exist for daily lessons as well as for units of instruction, the course, and the overall program. These outcomes emanate from basic questions about learners and how they learn. Instructors choose appropriate strategies and measure student learning against the specified outcomes. The entire process of instructional design forces instructors to focus on the intended outcomes of the lesson, exercise more choice in the delivery of instruction, and monitor each student's progress toward the outcomes. Figure 1.1 summarizes the characteristics of traditional and systematic instructional design.

In short, systematic instructional design changes how teachers plan, deliver, and monitor instruction. Three sets of questions frame the separate phases of instructional design:

1. **Planning:** What do students need to know? Why do they need to know it? What is important to teach? After instruction, what questions should students be able to ask

	Traditional Instruction	Systematic Instructional Design
Focus:	Teacher-centered	Student-centered
Instructional Goal:	To cover a certain amount of content	To build new student skills, knowledge, and attitudes
Structure:	Standardized curriculum and course syllabi	Performance outcomes developed at course and lesson level
Delivery:	Teacher-centered; minimal use of alternative teaching strategies	Student-centered; alternative teaching strategies
Assessment:	Content knowledge tests administered to all students	Individualized student monitoring of knowledge and performance gains
Evaluation:	Intra-group comparison of knowledge learned	Students are individually measured against performance standards

Figure 1.1 Comparison of traditional and systematic instructional design.

and answer? How will the learners be different after instruction?

2. **Instructional Delivery:** What is the best and most efficient way to teach this material? How will learners most effectively learn this material?

3. **Lesson Monitoring:** How do I know if the learner is learning? What must my students do to demonstrate that they have a thoughtful grasp of the material? What will successful students look like?

In this workbook we look at classroom instruction from the perspective of systematic instructional design. We emphasize the thought processes in which instructors engage as they make decisions about the appropriate strategies to deal effectively with the instructional needs of students. Learning does **not** take place in the same way and in the same time frame for all students. Standardized curricula, course syllabi, and teaching from textbooks are simply no longer sufficient for delivering instruction in an era of heightened expectations, specified performance outcomes, and concern for the individual's learning needs.

TRAITS OF EFFECTIVE INSTRUCTORS

Hyslop (1988, p. 19) and others have isolated traits that appear to be present in effective instructors. Among the more common traits often identified, effective instructors:

► Focus on the performance outcomes expected from the instruction.
► Have a genuine concern for and interest in learners.
► Maintain high expectations of learners and themselves.
► Have a deep commitment to teaching excellence and professional growth.
► Have subject matter expertise.
► Are enthusiastic, energetic, and possess excellent communications and human relations skills.
► Are flexible, innovative, and able to change methodology based upon the performance of learners.
► Understand teaching/learning styles as well as the differences between teaching adults and youth.
► Understand the importance of developing thinking skills in learners and the transfer of learning to other situations.
► Actively engage learners in lessons.

Such a list of traits can be useful to supervisors when they consider applicants for teaching positions and when they review current instructors. Identification of the traits in potential instructors may prevent hiring mistakes. Each trait also is an excellent topic for a faculty in-service program.

PERFORMANCE ACTIVITIES

1. Rate your institution on a scale of 1-5 (with 1 being the lowest) on each of the seven characteristics identified for effective schools. After completing the ratings, prepare a plan for your instructional supervisor detailing what you think the school must do to improve each of its ratings. Use Evaluation Form A for this activity (see Figure 1.2).

2. Choose one of your favorite instructors from your learning experiences and rate that person on a scale of 1-5 (with 1 being the lowest) on each of the ten traits of effective instructors. Use Evaluation Form B for this activity (see Figure 1.3).

3. Rate yourself on a scale of 1-5 (with 1 being the lowest) on each of the ten traits of effective instructors. Then prepare a plan for personal improvement in each area rated 3 or below.

4. Identify other characteristics of effective schools that you consider important. Rate your school on those characteristics and suggest ways of improvement.

5. Identify other traits you think are important in effective instructors. Rate yourself on the traits and develop a plan for improvement on any item rated 3 or below.

EVALUATION FORM A
Characteristics of Effective Schools

	Not at all		Moderately		To a Large Degree
Clear and focused mission which serves as the cornerstone for the instructional program	1	2	3	4	5
Instructional leader who has the responsibility of accomplishing the mission and who is a visible leader	1	2	3	4	5
High level of time on task in classroom	1	2	3	4	5
High expectations of students and staff	1	2	3	4	5
Frequent monitoring of student progress	1	2	3	4	5
Safe and orderly environment conducive to teaching and learning	1	2	3	4	5
Parental and community involvement in the school	1	2	3	4	5

Figure 1.2 Evaluation Form A.

EVALUATION FORM B
Traits of Effective Instructors

	Not at all		Moderately		To a Large Degree
Effective instructors focus on the performance outcomes expected from the instruction	1	2	3	4	5
Effective instructors have a genuine concern for and interest in learners	1	2	3	4	5
Effective instructors maintain high expectations of learners and themselves	1	2	3	4	5
Effective instructors have a deep commitment to excellence in teaching and to professional growth	1	2	3	4	5
Effective instructors have subject matter expertise	1	2	3	4	5
Effective instructors are enthusiastic, energetic, and possess excellent communications and human relations skills	1	2	3	4	5
Effective instructors are flexible, innovative, and able to change methodology based upon the performance of learners	1	2	3	4	5
Effective instructors understand teaching/learning styles as well as the differences between teaching adults and youth	1	2	3	4	5
Effective instructors understand the importance of developing thinking skills in learners and the transfer of learning to other situations	1	2	3	4	5
Effective instructors actively engage learners in the lesson	1	2	3	4	5

Figure 1.3 Evaluation Form B.

One must learn by doing the thing; for though you think you know it, you have no certainty until you try.

Sophocles

CURRICULUM/COURSE PLANNING

Most texts dealing with instructional methodology begin at the lesson level. However, before effective teachers can decide what to teach in a given lesson, they need to identify overall course outcomes (called objectives by many). Additionally, course outcomes must fit into the broader program the student will undertake. Educators sometimes use different terms to refer to the same instructional setting. For example, in some schools, the term **unit** means the same as **lesson** while in others it means **course**. For our purposes, we will use three terms: programs, courses, and lessons. An educational program prepares the students to enter a job and ranges in length from several weeks to two years. College- and university-level career programs are typically four or five years in length. Programs usually consist of 12 to 20 courses, and each course usually consists of 10 to 30 lessons (depending on how the teacher designs the lessons in terms of size and complexity).

There are many approaches to planning for program, course, and lesson outcomes. Perhaps the most logical is to first determine the major outcomes expected from the overall program (for example, accounting, computer programming, electronics). Major outcomes should be broad in nature and based on the actual requirements of the job. Industry requirements in a given field should be a foundation for determining program outcomes. Figure 2.1 shows examples of how educational outcomes parallel the requirements of the job. It is the instructor's job to design instruction to ensure that students meet the outcomes and measure student performance in relation to them.

Once the program outcomes are identified, the instructor must determine which courses are needed, how each course fits into the program, and how each course leads to successful completion of the broad program outcomes. The outcomes expected at the course level are broader than those at the lesson level but not as broad as those at the program level. Additionally, a formal evaluation component should be considered for course outcomes.

Course outcomes are authentic performance statements that build on and demand the integration of specific lesson outcomes. When students are required to put two or three new lesson skills together, they often must master a new and more difficult skill. An example of course level and lesson level outcomes is shown in Figure 2.2. In each case, the learner has

```
Program: Accounting                         Position: Accounting Information Clerk
```

- ► Prepare a statement of changes in financial position.

- ► Prepare payroll using PC for transmittal through modem to automated payroll service.

- ► Process transactions for a manufacturing business; prepare financial statements; adjust and close accounts.

- ► Account for the formation, operation, investments, and long-term liabilities of a corporation.

- ► Account for the operations and dissolution of a partnership.

```
Program: Telemarketing                      Position: Telemarketing Accounts Manager
```

- ► Develop dialogue scripts for a variety of sales calls.

- ► Sell or set up appointments to sell a company's product or service following the seven steps of a telemarketing call while employing effective telephone fluency skills.

- ► Provide service and information as required to customers and prospects following the seven steps of a telemarketing call while employing effective telephone fluency skills.

- ► Handle stressful calls under a variety of conflict situations.

- ► Maintain prospect and customer database or records for efficient call preparation, follow-up schedules, and status reports.

Figure 2.1 Examples of educational program outcomes based on requirements of the job. (Notice how each outcome resembles the statements on a job description.)

Program: Microapplications Specialist

Course Level Outcomes	Lesson Level Outcomes
Process business documents: letters, memos, reports	► Loads software and executes functions and commands of word processing software
	► Formats memos and letters
	► Uses word processing utilities for spell check and macros
Uses databases for storing, searching, and accessing records	► Creates records
	► Adds, deletes, and edits records
	► Sorts and searches data

Figure 2.2 Example of course level and lesson level outcomes.

to perform each lesson level outcome before he or she can perform the course outcome.

In planning course outcomes, the teacher must determine what students need to know about the content of the course and what they already know. It is helpful to examine other course syllabi in the same subject area.

Having identified major program and course outcomes, the instructor is now ready to identify how various lessons lead to those outcomes. At this level, it is especially important for the instructor to be able to measure the degree to which students have achieved the lesson performances. (Later in Chapter 2 we will discuss appropriate ways to write performance outcome statements.) Performances at the lesson level are typically subperformances of major course outcomes. An example of the flow from major course outcomes to lesson performances is shown in Figure 2.3.

To ensure that your instruction stays relevant and focused on your primary purpose, it is important to analyze the curriculum **from the opposite way your students will experience the curriculum**. To establish the primary outcomes of your course, ask yourself these questions: At the end of the course, what are the main ways the learners will be different? What are the most difficult new skills they will have learned? What significant new knowledge and performances will have been acquired?

Once you have defined your outcomes for the course, analyze each outcome and ask yourself: What does the learner need to know or do to satisfactorily perform the major outcome of the course? Say, for example, you are teaching a course on filing and the primary outcome is to establish filing systems for efficient document storage and access for three different office systems. Your analysis of the primary outcome reveals the following subperformances:

- ► establishes alphabetic and numeric files
- ► indexes and codes documents
- ► sorts documents alphabetically or numerically
- ► creates electronic directories and corresponding file names

Only after the student satisfactorily performs these subperformances will he or she be able to perform the terminal course outcome. By analyzing each of the main performances and determining the need-to-know information to reach that performance, instruction can be sequenced for learning efficiency and effectiveness. Figure 2.4 lays out the "backward" approach to curriculum planning.

Course Goal	Uses Microapplications Productivity Tools to Solve Business Problems		
Course Outcomes	Uses Word Processing	Uses Databases	Uses Spreadsheets
Lesson Outcomes	Loads software and executes functions and commands of word processing software	Creates records	Corrects formula errors
	Formats memos and letters	Adds, deletes, and edits records	Converts spreadsheet data to bar graphs
	Uses word processing utilities for spell check and macros	Sorts and searches data	Designs spreadsheet templates

Figure 2.3 Major course outcomes and performance outcomes.

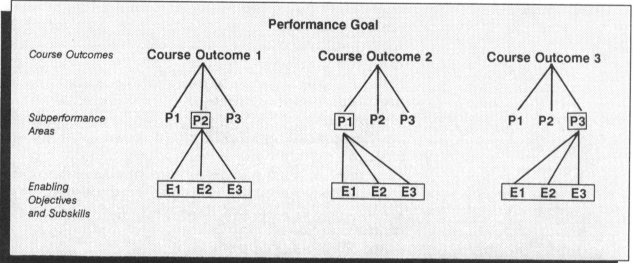

Figure 2.4 Analyzing your course curriculum using the "backward" approach. (Note that the curriculum is designed and developed opposite from the way learners experience the curriculum.)

If planning is being done in the manner described, teachers begin by identifying three to six major course outcomes. Each of these outcomes is then analyzed for required knowledge and skills (subperformances and topics) so that instruction remains focused and accountable. Next, as instructors prepare individual lesson plans, they make certain that students are building smaller skills into the major, authentic performances required by the major course outcomes.

Curriculum/course planning is an ongoing process. Too often, instructors rely upon a textbook publisher to provide the framework for individual courses and then teach from the text. The process should be exactly the opposite. Textbook selection should be based upon the predetermined outcomes of the instruction. Quality texts are organized around performance outcomes but do not dictate how the instruction is delivered or evaluated. Remember, textbooks do not teach; they are resources. Teachers teach!

Equally important is the understanding that no publisher can determine how an institution should measure performance outcomes. Curriculum development and evaluation need to be school based, and only the institution knows its available resources and school standards for excellence. Even though publishers often state major course outcomes in textbooks, it remains the responsibility of the individual instructor to plan for measurement of performance outcomes for both individual lessons and the entire course.

LESSON PLANNING: THE NEED FOR PERFORMANCE OUTCOMES

No serious educator would question the need for teaching to some objective or outcome. But what type of outcome? Most instructors have outcomes in mind before any given lesson. The unfortunate truth, however, is that many of the outcomes are not well focused. Only the most effective instructors clearly understand what the student should be able to do as a result of the instruction.

Gagne and Briggs (1979, p. 118) suggest that well-stated objectives (we are using the term **outcomes**) meet two needs. First, they communicate the purposes of instruction. Second, they affirm the need for evaluation of instruction. Troyer (1971, p. 44) suggests that the arrangement of processes and content into instructional sequences flows naturally from well-stated objectives.

By definition, any discussion of systematic instructional design includes development of performance outcomes. Since the main focus of systematic instructional design is on the learner, well-written outcome statements are an absolute necessity. But being able to properly state performance outcomes for individual lessons is only half of the equation. Of equal importance is monitoring whether those outcomes are being attained. Evaluation of performance outcomes is a natural outgrowth of a systematic instructional design system, as is the selection of supplementary resources and instructional methodology. In addition, active learning will occur with more regularity in lessons where the instructor appropriately states performance outcomes. Performance outcomes clearly tell students what is expected of them; as a result, they are able to monitor their own learning and recognize their learning needs.

WRITING PERFORMANCE OUTCOME STATEMENTS

There are several accepted methods of writing performance outcome statements for individual lessons. Gagne and Briggs

(1979, p. 120) suggest five components to a well-written performance outcome statement: situation, learned capability, object, action, and tools/constraints. Troyer (1971, p. 48) suggests three components: situation, behavioral terms, and acceptance level. The former National Center for Research in Vocational Education at Ohio State University (1987, N-4, p. 22) also suggests three components: performance required, conditions under which it will be performed, and criteria to be met. Harris, Hillenmeyer, and Foran (1989, p. 47) suggest four components: a stimulus phrase, an action verb, criteria describing acceptable performance or production, and stipulated conditions of and materials for performance and production.

A closer look at these four methods for writing performance outcome statements suggests there is really little difference among them. Despite differences in terminology, these authors and many others agree on the basics. Since the intent of this workbook is to simplify educational theory to the extent possible, we will use a three-step approach to writing performance outcome statements. You will quickly observe, however, that the elements mentioned by other authors exist within the three steps. Remember that there are two basic reasons for writing performance outcome statements: to communicate the expected outcomes from instruction and to affirm the need to evaluate instruction.

The three steps we will use throughout this workbook are as follows:

1. Express or state the performance outcome using a verb and direct object.
2. Provide the situation in which the student will perform the desired behavior or performance.
3. Include the criteria that describe acceptable performance and conditions of performance.

Performance

The first component of the performance outcome statement is the actual expected performance. Typically it consists of an action verb and direct object. The instructor should use action verbs that allow for an independent third party to observe whether the behavior actually occurred. Often the words **should be able to, shall,** or **will** precede the action verb.

Verbs that describe behaviors not easily observed (for example, **know, appreciate,** or **understand**) are inappropriate. Certainly instructors want students to understand or appreciate various aspects of presented material. However, we cannot adequately measure these verbs, so instructors should not use them in performance outcome statements. Verbs such as **demonstrate, identify, classify, execute,** and **choose** are examples of observable behaviors and hence are acceptable action verbs for performance outcomes. The direct object of the stated performance follows the action verb. Here is an example of a correctly stated action verb and direct object: **will identify ten characteristics**.

The following list of observable action verbs (Scannell and Tracy, 1975, p. 44) can be helpful.

add	define	identify	prove
analyze	describe	interpret	record
assemble	diagram	itemize	rewrite
bisect	disassemble	list	sing
build	dissect	locate	solve
calculate	divide	make	subtract
choose	draw	measure	summarize
compare	explain	multiply	support
construct	extract	outline	tell
contrast	extrapolate	play	translate
correct	factor	predict	weigh
criticize	graph	produce	write

Situation

The second part of a well-written performance outcome statement provides the situation in which the student will perform the desired behavior. Usually it includes a stimulus phrase that focuses the student's response. Often the stimulus phrase begins with words such as **when presented with, using,** or **in response to**. A well-stated stimulus phrase relates directly to the evaluation of the performance outcome. It does not simply describe the treatment to be endured, since that treatment is not nearly as important as the performance required. Hence, **after reading this text,** is an unclear situation component: it simply describes what the student will have read, not the problem to be confronted. In contrast, the phrase **when presented with five chemicals,** is an acceptable situation component. Other acceptable situation phrases include: **given a problem of this type** and **provided a standard set of tools and a DC motor that contains a malfunction.**

Criteria and Conditions

The third component of a well-written performance outcome statement stipulates the criteria for acceptable performance and the conditions for the performance. Stated properly, the criteria component removes any confusion about the performance expected. The statement may be a separate sentence or part of the sentence containing the situation and performance. The criteria should be clear enough for an independent observer to assess whether the performance occurred to the degree expected. Here are examples of acceptable criteria statements: **with 90 percent accuracy,** and **to industry standards specified on the employability test.**

Conditions often reflect considerations such as time limits, special materials, or special equipment required or excluded. Here are two examples of conditions: **using the binomial theorem** and **within thirty minutes**. The instructor should take special care not to add so many conditions that the outcome is not easily observed or that it fails because of being cumbersome.

Evaluating Statements

Now that we have reviewed the three components of a well-written performance outcome statement, let us look at a few examples of poorly written components.

Weak situation component:

▶ After completing the laboratory experiment . . .
▶ Having viewed the video . . .

These components are weak because the situation in each does not relate to a method of evaluation. In addition, neither mentions an authentic or realistic problem the learner will face. Each component merely states the treatment to be endured; that is, the instructional activity.

Weak performance component:

▶ . . . will understand the causes . . .
▶ . . . shall be able to appreciate the beauty . . .

The weakness in both of these components is the use of unobservable action verbs. **Understand** could mean simple awareness or in-depth comprehension. Likewise, **appreciate** covers too wide a spectrum of possibilities for useful instructional planning.

Weak criteria component:

▶ . . . minimum accepted performance is answering enough correctly to demonstrate understanding.

The weakness in this criteria component is that it is virtually impossible to demonstrate understanding without additional, clearly explained criteria.

▶ . . . acceptable level of performance is achieved when the learner compares and contrasts the six characteristics.

This criteria component is weak because there is no basis for comparison that an independent third party could observe with any level of accuracy.

> ▸ ..., using the drafting board, mechanical pencils, and other instruments, making certain to complete the project within twenty-seven minutes and folding the paper in half when done ...

There are too many conditions attached to this criteria component. The outcome will not be understood or will fail because of its own weight.

Now let us look at two performance outcome statements that have much more clearly stated components.

> ▸ When presented with ten linear equations (situation), the learner will identify the unknown variable (performance) using the addition/subtraction method (condition). Acceptable performance level is 80 percent accuracy (criteria).
> ▸ When presented with five sample business letters, each written with ten capitalization, punctuation, and grammatical usage errors (situation), the student will correct the letters (performance) using guidelines taught in class from *Business Communications: A Problem-Solving Approach*, sixth edition (condition). Acceptable performance is 95 percent accuracy (criteria).

In sum, properly stated performance outcome statements serve as guidelines for the choices instructors must make in the delivery of instruction. These choices might include instructional materials, equipment, modes of instruction, and methods of assessment. Most important, outcomes focus the lesson on the learner rather than on the instructor or the content.

Although each lesson might have related or secondary outcomes, the primary one should be of such significance that without it, the lesson would be of no consequence. Outcomes should be at the appropriate level of difficulty. In some lessons the instructor will not inform the students of the outcome because of the nature of the lesson itself. It is always the prerogative of the teacher to either state the outcome and guide students toward it or to set up an inductive or discovery lesson and help students discover the outcome by the end of the lesson. Remember, even an unclear performance outcome statement is better than none. However, clearly written outcome statements maximize the potential for the lesson to have meaning and for learners to achieve expected results.

Regardless of which method the instructor chooses to write performance outcome statements, the most important aspects are the same: the simplicity and clarity with which they are written and the ability for them to be observed easily and independently.

PERFORMANCE ACTIVITIES

1. Review the statements listed below. Indicate which of the statements are **actual** performances that can be demonstrated. That is, which ones tell **what** the learner is **expected to do**? (To help you focus on just the performance, conditions and criteria of acceptable performance were not included.)

STATEMENTS: A performance or not?

a. Write the symbols for any 20 electronic components.
b. Demonstrate an understanding of business communications.
c. Show a knowledge of the basic elements of a contract.
d. Take and record blood pressure for an adult patient of any size or weight.
e. Use each function key of a 10-key calculator correctly when solving a series of problems.
f. Demonstrate competency in job search skills.
g. Appreciate the different learning styles of students.
h. Use utilities for electronic document communications.
i. Prepare a statement of changes in financial position.
j. Deal with issues concerning human relations, recruitment, and hiring.
k. Compose business memos at the keyboard.
l. Discuss principles and techniques of computer programming.
m. Write and test a program to calculate arithmetic means.

PERFORMANCE ACTIVITIES (Continued)

n. Develop a critical understanding of the importance of leadership.

o. Apply scientific knowledge to solve environmental problems.

p. Participate in a job interview.

q. Discuss the importance of motivation.

r. Configure an IBM PC system: monitor, drives, CPU, and printer.

s. Outline the proper steps to follow in establishing a records management system.

2. Review the performances listed below. Indicate which ones would be expected for end-of-course perform- ances and which ones are "lesson level" performances. (To help you focus on just the performance, conditions and criterion of acceptable performance were not included.)

a. Read a domestic electric power meter correctly to the nearest unit and record the reading on the meter reader's log.

b. Type a business letter in accordance with the standards described in the Company Manual 12-21.

c. Using a metric balance, measure to the nearest gram.

d. Relate and align job requirements to program curriculum content.

e. Remove and replace any engine part on the XYZ model of a single-engine airplane.

f. Discriminate between normal and abnormal X-rays.

g. Identify the 10 tools used for winding mainsprings.

h. Compute the discount rate to the nearest whole percent based on the original and current sale price.

i. Identify transistors on a schematic diagram.

j. Repair an amplifier unit so that it functions within design specifications.

k. Record payroll and payroll tax expenses.

l. Account for the dissolution of a partnership.

m. Develop an effective telemarketing record management system.

PERFORMANCE ACTIVITIES (Continued)

n. Recognize the difference between pronunciation and articulation.

o. Develop dialogue scripts for a variety of types of telephone sales calls.

p. Classify business items as either assets, liabilities, or owner's equity.

q. Design a combination journal with 11 special money columns for recording the transactions in a medical practice.

r. Describe the uses of word processing software.

3. For any one of the courses you teach, specify the primary goal or outcome of the course. Then determine three to six major performance outcomes. For each of these major outcomes, identify at least two main subperformances within those outcomes. As an example of a main performance outcome, refer to Figure 2.2.

4. For each course you teach, write three properly stated performance outcome statements using three separate lessons from the first month of the course.

5. Review the performance outcome statements written by a colleague in response to Performance Activity 4. Prepare a written critique for each statement. Share your critique with the colleague.

CHAPTER 3   TEACHING

It is nothing short of a miracle that modern methods of instruction have not yet entirely strangled the holy curiosity of inquiry.

Albert Einstein

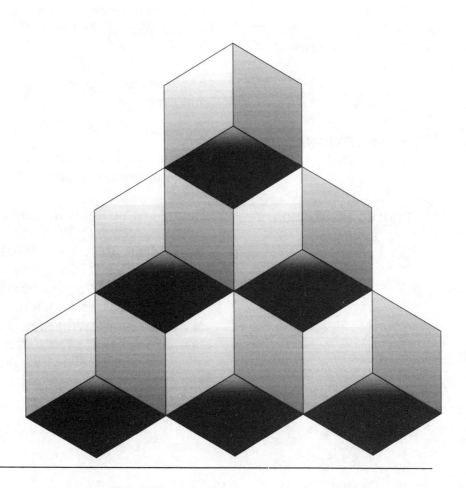

SECTION I:
DELIVERING RELEVANT INSTRUCTION

AN ART OR A SCIENCE?

Is teaching an art or a science? Perhaps a little of both? If teaching is purely a science, then universal principles exist and precise adherence to them would in all probability lead to learning. If teaching is an art, then it relies largely on the skill of the performer (instructor) to deliver the message effectively.

Certainly enough research exists on teaching and learning to provide a scientific framework. But it is extremely unlikely that a responsible educator would suggest that the mere application of a framework by itself leads to effective teaching. Anyone who has ever taught realizes that even the best plans and systems go awry when confronted by real, live students. Instant and frequent decision making becomes an absolute requirement for the effective instructor. The ability to adjust spontaneously to situations as they arise is perhaps the most important ingredient to success in the classroom.

Hence, we will consider teaching to be both a science and an art. As a science, effective teaching follows certain time-tested and research-based principles. Since the individual instructor must adapt and choose various courses of action based on learner feedback, we also view teaching as an art form. Teaching is an art that should be appreciated and respected for its complexity and reliance upon individual effort and expertise.

INSTRUCTIONAL DECISIONS

All effective instructors make a variety of decisions at each step of the instructional process.

Prior to Instruction

Before instruction even takes place, the instructor makes many content decisions. What content is appropriate and important for students to learn? What do my students already know about this area? How much time do I need to allocate to any given portion of the lesson? How should I group the students? What activities and materials should I use? How should I assess learning? What are my strengths as an instructor, and how do I maximize those strengths for the benefit of students? What principles of learning will I emphasize? Will I have enough activities to deal with the various learning styles of my students? How can I get my students to think rather than simply recite?

During Instruction

Once instruction begins, the instructor makes an entirely new set of decisions. Am I monitoring whether and what students are learning? What success rate am I achieving? Am I asking appropriate questions, and am I receiving acceptable responses? Do I need to adjust the lesson based upon feedback I am getting from learners? Are learners achieving the performance outcomes? If not, do I need to change the pace of the lesson? Are the learners ready for independent practice? Do I need to take an entirely different approach?

After Instruction

Finally, there are a variety of decisions the instructor makes after the lesson. What do I need to do to evaluate the performance of learners? How can I facilitate the transfer of learning regarding today's lesson? What types of remediation and follow-up activities are needed? How can I provide positive feedback to learners to enhance further achievement? What are my next steps?

Even a casual reader can see that the life of a classroom instructor is full of critical decisions. The events of any instructional model always depend on the ability of the individual instructor to monitor and adjust to situations that arise in the classroom.

PRINCIPLES OF LEARNING

In making the variety of decisions necessary for an effective lesson, instructors must remember some basic principles of learning. At the very least, the following principles need to be considered.

Feedback

The term **feedback** can be used in a variety of ways. Some authors use it to indicate the communication that exists between teacher and students. Others use it to indicate whether the teacher understands the degree to which students have learned. In our discussions, we will use the former description — communication between teacher and students. Feedback from students is critically important. Only through feedback do you know if your students are paying attention and understanding the lesson.

Motivation

True motivation does not attempt to find ways to **make** a student learn. Rather, it ensures that appropriate circumstances exist in the environment so students want to learn. Controlling motivational variables is one of the primary tasks of the instructor. Hunter (1980, *Motivation*, p. 7) suggests that two important variables in motivation deal with the learner's feelings: (1) the instructor's degree of concern for or tension with the learner and (2) the instructor's "feeling tone" with the learner.

Hunter also suggests four task-related variables that increase motivation: (1) the degree to which the task interests the learner, (2) success in performing the task, (3) feedback from the instructor, and (4) knowledge of results. Finally, Hunter suggests that the mere performance of a task which is itself rewarding to the individual is motivational.

Perhaps the greatest motivation for students, however, is effective classroom instruction. If the instructor is able to create an environment in which students receive clear messages that they can learn, can experience success, and can be actively involved in each lesson, student motivation becomes much less of a problem.

Reinforcement

Reinforcement is anything that strengthens or encourages the desired response. It is a message from the instructor to the learner that indicates pleasure or displeasure with the learner's behavior. In positive reinforcement, the instructor rewards or praises the learner for acceptable behavior. In negative reinforcement, the instructor usually issues some type of punishment for inappropriate behavior. Instructors may also attempt to eliminate (often called extinguish) negative behavior by providing no reinforcement whatsoever; essentially they ignore the behavior.

Practice

Guided and independent practice are essential tools in the delivery of instruction. The instructor must first show learners how to solve a particular problem, check their understanding, guide them through their first practice problems, and then provide the opportunity for the learner to proceed independently. At this point the instructor is able to further assess the performance of individual learners. The type and amount of practice afforded students are two important variables in student achievement.

Transfer of Learning

Hunter (1980, *Teach for Transfer*, p. 1) suggests that teaching for transfer should be the goal of all teaching. Unless a learner is able to transfer past learning to learning in the present situation, the value of either is suspect. During the planning stages, the instructor must consider how the lesson will help develop critical thinking and problem-solving skills, which are at the very heart of transfer of learning. Focusing on the ability to generalize the results of a particular lesson is certainly one way of increasing these skills. Students need to learn not only the type of problems presented in class but also new problems with slightly different conditions or questions.

Sequencing Instruction

Course and lesson sequencing are critical components of learning in systematic instructional design. The major performance outcomes of the course need to be sequenced and listed in a logical and sound instructional order. The sequencing of lessons should correspond to the subperformances in each area. Sequencing of lessons should also take into account the learning styles of the students and the teaching style of the instructor. Instruction is most effective when the instructor provides it in meaningful chunks, with the chunks making a coherent whole. Pacing of the chunks is also important to the overall effectiveness of the lesson.

Typically lesson sequencing proceeds in one of the following manners: from the known to the unknown, from the simple to the complex, from the concrete to the abstract, from the particular to the general, from observations to reasoning, or from the whole to the parts and back to the whole again.

Retention

Learners retain more information when they participate actively in a lesson that has meaning for them. Retention is also improved if the instructor is able to relate subject matter to previously learned material so a bridge between concepts is clear. Practice is another significant variable in retention. Indeed, research indicates that students need overpractice to truly retain a new concept or skill.

Time on Task

Considerable research exists about the importance of time on task, or engaged time, in the classroom. Unnecessary interruptions to the instructional process should be avoided. Instructors must not waste valuable time by engaging in nonproductive activities.

LEARNING STYLES

In making the variety of daily decisions that are critical to learning, the instructor must focus on the various learning styles of the students in the class. The interaction of these learning styles with the teaching style of the instructor creates a productive climate in the classroom.

Learning styles typically fall into three categories: visual, auditory, and kinesthetic. Visual learners, as the term implies, enjoy receiving information through any method that stimulates the visual senses. They enjoy reading books, solving puzzles, and watching videos. Often they are quiet in class. The demonstration mode of instruction is particularly effective with the visual learner.

Auditory learners enjoy receiving information through hearing. Consequently, these learners tend to be talkative. They enjoy stories and other spoken material more than visual information. Auditory learners generally are able to handle lectures and group work very well. They also learn well from videos if the sound is of good quality.

Kinesthetic learners enjoy learning through touching. They do not like sitting still for long periods of time. They work best with their hands and enjoy skill-type activities. Kinesthetic learners do quite well in laboratory settings.

Consider any typical classroom (or for that matter your own family) and you will observe a wide range of learning styles. Similarly, since each teacher is also a learner with an individual learning style, that style tends to dominate the teaching as well as the learning. The important point for instructors to realize is that these factors exist, and then to plan accordingly. The instructor who delivers the same type of lesson using the same teaching methodology every day is simply cheating students. Effective teachers stretch their personal style and use a variety of modes of instruction to enhance learning in the classroom.

ADULT/YOUTH LEARNING

Instructors must also understand that differences in the age of the learners require adjustments in teaching strategies. Adult learners want practical applications in their studies. They are generally impatient with philosophical presentations, unless it is made clear how such information affects their lives. Adults usually learn well from peers, and the effective use of time is important to them. Adults also often enjoy discovery learning rather than simply being provided with information. They tend to learn more slowly than youth, but, nevertheless, learn equally well. Finally, adults tend to be internally motivated, self-directed, and intolerant of information that contradicts well-established beliefs.

In teaching youth, instructors need to keep in mind that younger learners need much more support than adults. They generally learn what they are told, often without question. They have little appreciation for time, and they are motivated by external rewards. Younger learners, because of their limited knowledge and experience base, are usually more open to new ideas. They also tend to adjust easily to new situations.

EVENTS OF INSTRUCTION

Many authors have attempted to provide specific steps for a typical classroom lesson. Unfortunately, some educators have adopted these steps as an ironclad recipe for effective instruction. Some have gone so far as to base instructor evaluation on the presence or absence of such steps.

At the outset, let us dispel the notion that each lesson has exactly the same steps. Such a declaration violates a basic premise of instructional design — that instructors must constantly adapt and make spontaneous decisions in the classroom based upon student performance. In making these decisions, any one of the recommended steps may not appear in a given lesson. The operative word is **results**. Instructors change the process as they teach in order to achieve the desired results. This reality is what makes the teaching profession so demanding and complex.

Despite the problems inherent in suggesting that typical lessons contain similar steps, we must ensure that the illusion of learning in the classroom does not replace the reality of its occurrence. Considerable research exists that identifies practices that tend to facilitate learning. Instructors who use these practices judiciously and on a regular basis increase the likelihood that students will achieve the desired results.

What are the practices that generally allow effective instruction? Is it possible to classify them into a model that, if not applied too rigidly, enhances student performance? Many authors respond to that question in the affirmative. Hunter (1984, p. 175) developed a model that suggests seven parts to effective lessons:

1. The anticipatory set (focusing student attention)
2. Objectives and purpose
3. Input (identification of knowledge and skills required)
4. Modeling (instructor models the desired behavior)
5. Checking for understanding
6. Guided practice
7. Independent practice

Gagne and Briggs (1979, p. 157) suggest nine steps for a typical lesson:

1. Gaining attention
2. Informing the learner of the objective
3. Stimulating recall of prerequisite learnings
4. Presenting the stimulus material
5. Providing learning guidance
6. Eliciting the performance
7. Providing feedback about performance correctness
8. Assessing the performance
9. Enhancing retention and transfer

Although the terminology differs between the Gagne and Briggs model and the Hunter model, the substance is remarkably similar. That similarity should not be particularly surprising, however, since both models emanate from considerable research.

Rosenshine (1982, pp. 7-25) suggests six important steps in a typical lesson:

1. Checking the previous day's work and reteaching if necessary
2. Presentation of the material
3. Initial student practice
4. Feedback and corrections
5. Independent practice
6. Weekly and monthly reviews

As with the other authors, Rosenshine believes that these lesson steps are crucial for instructors at all levels and learners of any age.

In an effort to provide a simplified instructional model, we will use a three-step approach to a typical classroom lesson as suggested by Davies (1981). You will quickly observe, however, that all of the steps included in the other models are present in our model. They simply do not exist in separate, distinguishable steps. The three steps in our model are: introduction, development, and consolidation.

Step 1: Introduction

During the introductory stage of a typical lesson, many things occur. Essentially, the instructor is attempting to prepare the learners for the lesson. The first important component of this effort is getting the attention of the learners. The instructor is able to accomplish this task in a variety of ways: asking a provocative or startling question, providing introductory exercises on the chalkboard, relating a story or incident, and appealing to the learners' interests in some way. The important point is getting the learners' undivided attention so the lesson may have its intended impact.

The next component of the introduction is stating the performance outcome(s) of the lesson. If the lesson is one of discovery, the instructor may want the learners to discover the outcome of the lesson as the lesson develops. Students should be able to ask questions about the outcome and why it is important. Therefore, the instructor must make the purpose of the outcome as clear as the statement itself. It is important for students to know what they will do to accomplish the performance outcome. They must also understand how they will know that they have succeeded in achieving the desired results.

In the final part of the introductory stage of the lesson, the instructor informs learners, or elicits from them, the ways in which the new lesson relates to previously learned material or what they already know about the topic. This may also be the appropriate time to check the previous day's work so students see some connection between the lessons. Since instructors usually present units in chunks, learners must understand how those chunks fit into a bigger picture. Thus not only is the recall of previously learned material important for purposes of retention, but it is critical so that learners can transfer previous learning to the present situation. In the process, learners are developing some of the most important skills of all — the ability to think critically, synthesize information, and solve problems.

Step 2: Development

The developmental stage of the instructional model, which has several parts, involves presentation of new material. The instructor must make a number of decisions, including the choice of the most appropriate mode(s) of instruction to deliver the lesson. Often a combination of modes is the most effective approach. The choice, however, depends upon several factors: content of the lesson, learning styles of the students, teaching style of the instructor, available resources, and performance outcome of the lesson.

Among the more common choices of instructional modes are lecture, demonstration, small groups, laboratory, debate, discovery, games, audio/visual, independent study, simulation, review, oral questioning, computers, field trips, panel discussion, team teaching, projects, and work-study. Regardless of the choice(s) for any given lesson, the key is variety. Effective instructors realize that taking the same approach to instruction all the time will necessarily be less beneficial to some learners because of their individual learning styles. Consequently, instructors must use as many techniques as possible throughout an entire course and even in a given lesson.

In another part of the development stage of a lesson, the instructor provides guided and independent practice for learners. Research indicates that nothing is truly learned until it becomes embedded in long-term memory. Practice to the point of overlearning is essential. Guided practice occurs when the instructor leads the learners through a problem, demonstration, and so on. Throughout the guided practice, the instructor constantly checks for understanding by asking appropriate questions. Once the instructor believes that the learners have mastered the concepts, he or she allows them to practice independently to increase their likelihood of retention. During independent practice, the instructor assists individuals, provides feedback, and assesses the degree to which the performance outcome(s) is being met.

Step 3: Consolidation

The final stage in a typical lesson is consolidation. If assessment during independent practice or at other stages of the lesson has not already indicated the degree to which students have achieved the performance outcome, the instructor should make such an assessment at this time. The assessment should, of course, relate directly back to the well-stated performance outcome.

The consolidation stage of the lesson should include a brief review of the major points in the lesson. In addition to relating the lesson to previously learned material, the instructor should elicit from learners suggestions for applying the lesson's performance outcome to other situations. As with the introductory stage, this part of the lesson is extremely important in the development of critical thinking skills, the ability to synthesize information, and the ability to solve problems. Throughout the consolidation stage, retention and transfer of learning are of primary importance.

The time allotted to any one of the three steps in a lesson will vary based upon the type of lesson and mode of instruction selected. For example, in a knowledge-type lesson, the introduction and consolidation might be short, whereas the lecture or development might be lengthy. In a skill-type lesson, the introduction and demonstration or development might be relatively short, whereas the imitation or consolidation might be considerably longer. Once again, these are but a few of the wide variety of decisions instructors must make on a daily basis. Figure 3.1 summarizes the primary events in each stage of a lesson.

PLANNING

Planning an effective lesson is a skill required of all instructors. Without an effective plan, the lesson simply will not maximize learning. As important as this planning activity is, however, it is also critical for instructors to understand that the plan is nothing more than a guide. The real skill comes into play as the lesson develops. Through monitoring learner progress, the instructor constantly adjusts the plan to meet the needs of the situation as it evolves. Unfortunately, too many instructors are able to write beautiful lesson plans but simply do not have the skill to achieve the desired results.

What then are the elements of an effective plan? In keeping with our three-step model for an effective lesson, the

Introduction	Development	Consolidation
Attract learner's attention	Present new material	Review major points of lesson
State performance outcome	Model performance outcome	Synthesize lesson
State purpose of lesson	Provide guided practice	Teach for transfer to new problems
Relate lesson to previous material	Provide independent practice	Elicit modeling from students
Relate content to learner's prior knowledge	Elicit feedback from students	Evaluate learning
Relate content to "big picture"	Assess progress toward outcome	Diagnose and reteach if necessary

Figure 3.1 Characteristics of the introduction, development, and consolidation phases of effective lessons.

plan is relatively simple to develop. Using the outline shown in Figure 3.2 as a guide, an instructor can develop a lesson plan for any type of lesson.

CLASSROOM MANAGEMENT

Knowing the steps that make an effective lesson and how to plan for that lesson will be of no consequence if the instructor is unable to manage the classroom. Effective classroom

---

Lesson Plan

Course: _____   Lesson: _____

Date: _____   Lesson Outcome: _____

Special Equipment/Materials Required: _____

I.   Introduction

    A.   Attention: How will I get the students' attention?

    B.   Performance outcome(s) and purpose: What do I want the students to be able to do as a result of this lesson? Why should they be able to do it?

    C.   Prior knowledge: How does previously learned material relate to what we will do today? Is there previous work to be checked? What do students already know about this area?

II.   Development

    A.   Mode(s): What mode(s) of instruction will I use?

    B.   Activities: What sequence of activities will I use? When will I model the intended outcome?

    C.   Guided practice: How will I lead the class in applying the new information or skill?

    D.   Independent practice: What similar applications will I expect students to be able to make on their own? How much practice will students need? How can I arrange more practice if students need it? How will I elicit feedback from learners?

III.   Consolidation

    A.   Assessment: How will I know if the students achieved the performance outcome?

    B.   Review: What are the main points of the lesson that I need to review?

    C.   Transfer: What can I do to get students to think critically about today's lesson--how it relates to previously learned material and how it fits into the "big picture"?

    D.   Evaluation: How will I reteach if the lesson was unsuccessful? How will I motivate learners to "re-attempt" the lesson?

Figure 3.2   Guide for developing lesson plans.

---

management results in increased student involvement and decreased time off task. Hence, understanding and developing classroom management skills is of utmost importance to an effective instructor. Although teachers tend to use techniques that have proved successful for them in previous experiences, there are common elements of successful classroom management:

- Clear performance outcomes
- High expectations of students
- Clear directions to students
- Concern with student success (providing activities that work)
- Frequent monitoring of student progress (checking assignments daily and returning them to students)
- Frequent assignment of grades
- Clear criteria for student grades
- Notebooks maintained by students with assignment sheet, class papers, and notes
- Clear classroom rules
- Immediate and consistent handling of behavior problems
- Regular recognition of student achievement
- Active instruction and learning, rather than seat work
- Emphasis on time on task
- Instructor as role model

PERFORMANCE ACTIVITIES

1. Using the lesson plan format provided in Figure 3.2, prepare three detailed lesson plans for each course you teach.
2. Review the lesson plans written by a colleague in response to Performance Activity 1. Prepare a written critique for each of those plans. Share your critique with your colleague.

SECTION II:
ORAL QUESTIONING TECHNIQUES

BACKGROUND

Why devote a separate section to oral questioning techniques? Everyone knows asking questions has been part of teaching since the time of Socrates.

The reason is simple. Even though instructors understand the importance of asking effective questions, research shows that questioning does not always occur. Barnes (1983, pp. 61-81) claims that faculty often blame learners for lack of participation and passivity in the classroom when in fact the instructors themselves are a large part of the problem. Based upon observations in forty college classrooms, Barnes states that only 3.65 percent of the classroom time was spent in questioning. If that percentage is not alarming enough, consider that 63 percent of those questions were simple recall-type questions, and less than 5 percent could be classified as divergent-thinking or evaluative-type questions. If these data are at all similar in other sectors of education, is there any wonder why our students can't think for themselves?

Why is asking effective questions so important? Most experts agree that students learn better by doing or in active participation. Active participation, however, goes beyond simply doing. It includes the consistent involvement of the minds as well as the bodies of the learners. The easiest way to achieve this mental engagement is through questions that require the learner to think. The value of such thinking is that as it is being rehearsed in short-term memory, it is being retained and transferred to long-term memory. Active participation increases true learning. Active participation also provides the instructor with a tool for determining the degree to which students are meeting performance outcomes. Finally, it is an efficient way to monitor learner progress and adjust lessons accordingly.

LEVELS OF QUESTIONS

In order to understand the various levels of questions available to instructors, let us review Bloom's *Taxonomy of Educational Objectives* (Bloom, 1956). Bloom's taxonomy is a classification system for the various levels of the thinking processes. An understanding of this taxonomy is indispensable for any effective instructor. It guides instructors in specifying performance outcomes and it leads them to ask more effective questions, resulting in increased learning.

The taxonomy has six levels:

1. Knowledge
2. Comprehension
3. Application
4. Analysis
5. Synthesis
6. Evaluation

The knowledge level is the first stage of the taxonomy. It is essentially a recall of facts, definitions, or other memorized information. Knowledge is associated with remembering and it is the simplest form of the thinking processes. Too often inexperienced instructors stop here in preparing questions for learners. Answers to knowledge-type questions often consist of one word and are narrow in scope. Such a question has only one correct answer. Verbs usually found in this type of question include **name, define, locate, repeat, state,** and **recognize.** Questions usually begin with **who** or **what.**

Comprehension is the second level of the taxonomy. This stage of the thinking processes is slightly broader than the knowledge level; it requires the learner to select among facts, organize those facts, and restate them in the learner's own words. Comprehension connotes understanding. Questions at this level also tend to be quite narrow because there is only one correct answer. That answer usually takes the form of explaining, relating, or retelling. Verbs often used in framing comprehension questions include **discuss, describe, estimate, give examples, identify,** and **summarize.** Questions frequently begin with **why** or **who.**

The third level of the taxonomy is application. At this stage the learner must use information or skills learned. The operative word is **apply,** and the verbs often found with this level include **translate, interpret, employ, illustrate, schedule, solve,** and **show.** Simply stated, this level emphasizes the application of facts, rules, and principles to other situations.

The fourth level of the taxonomy is analysis, which is characterized by classification and sorting. Analysis-type questions use verbs such as **categorize, differentiate, compare, contrast,** and **criticize.** These questions involve the separation of the whole into it various parts. Analysis-type questions often begin with **how** or **what.**

The fifth level of Bloom's taxonomy is synthesis. At this level the learner combines ideas from previous learning to create a new whole. Synthesis is characterized by bringing together a variety of ideas or concepts. Verbs often found in synthesis-type questions include **compose, assemble, construct, organize, design, develop,** and **create.**

The sixth and final level of the taxonomy is evaluation. At this level of the thinking processes the learner develops opinions, judgments, or decisions based upon previously known facts or opinions. Verbs found in evaluation-type questions include **appraise, evaluate, prioritize, assess, decide, choose, select, justify,** and **recommend.** An evaluative-type question will often begin with **why** or **why not.**

In some of the literature, authors refer to only four steps of the thinking processes. In addition to the knowledge and evaluation levels used by Bloom, they use the terms **convergent thinking** and **divergent thinking** as the other two stages. Even though these two stages differ from Bloom's labels, convergent and divergent thinking certainly exist in his analysis and synthesis levels. We will discuss them here simply for information and comparative purposes, not because we wish to classify the thinking processes in this manner.

Convergent thinking refers to putting facts together and constructing an answer. Since these types of questions require one best answer, they are narrow in scope. Often a convergent question is characterized by the verbs **explain, state, translate, associate, compare, contrast,** and **conclude.** Divergent questions, on the other hand, require the learner to organize elements of previous learning into new patterns. These types of questions are much broader than convergent questions because they require learner originality and creativity in the learner's response. Verbs used in these questions include **elaborate, synthesize, infer, predict,** and **hypothesize.** There is obvious overlap between the convergent/divergent thinking levels and the comprehension, application, analysis, and synthesis levels of Bloom's taxonomy.

Now let us look as some examples of questions or directions related to the six levels of the thinking processes.

1. **Knowledge:** A. What dramatic event caused the United States to enter World War II? B. Define marketing.
2. **Comprehension:** A. Describe the damage that the Japanese caused to the U.S. Navy at Pearl Harbor. B. Describe the basic purposes of a marketing system.
3. **Application:** A. How is Pearl Harbor an example of the need for preparedness? B. How is the lite beer phenomenon an example of market segmentation?
4. **Analysis:** A. Compare and contrast the relative strengths of the U.S. Navy and the Japanese Navy immediately following Pearl Harbor. B. Compare the views of a typical marketing director with those of a quality assurance director in terms of marketing's effect on product quality.

5. **Synthesis:** A. Given the facts of Pearl Harbor, design an overall strategic defense that will eliminate such an attack in the future. B. Given the statistical data in the enclosed report, prepare an overall marketing plan for the company; include strategies and tactics.
6. **Evaluation:** A. Would you have dropped the bomb on Hiroshima? Why or why not? B. Given these two strategic marketing plans for our company, determine which would be more effective. Why?

STRATEGY FOR ASKING EFFECTIVE QUESTIONS

Being able to develop effective questions is not sufficient. Since questioning should encourage, direct, and extend thinking, the response to the question and the follow-up questions are as important as the original question itself. Without eliciting the appropriate response, the question fails in its major purpose. The strategy for asking questions is as important as the ability to frame questions properly.

Unfortunately, it is the strategy for asking questions that is often the biggest problem for a beginning instructor. The intent of asking questions should be to increase the quantity and quality of active learner participation. The experienced instructor realizes that using simple techniques will allow this participation to occur:

Teacher Behaviors

► Ask fewer, more simply worded questions.
► Ask follow-up, stepping-stone-type questions that get at different levels of difficulty.
► Distribute questions among all learners. Do not simply rely upon volunteers.
► Ask the question of the entire class, pause for at least three seconds, then call on a student to respond. After the response, pause again before commenting. This technique is critical, but it is commonly lacking in the inexperienced teacher. If an instructor designates a student before asking the question, the other students will "escape" without thinking. The initial pause creates productive anxiety by forcing learners to pay attention. The pause after the response stimulates further thinking.
► Praise and reinforce correct responses.
► Do not answer your own questions for students. If a student gives an incorrect response, rephrase the question or probe further. Be certain to explain why the answer given was wrong.
► Withhold judgment. Do not immediately evaluate learner responses.
► Help create energy in the classroom by moving around the room.

Student Behaviors

- Do not allow an excessive amount of hand waving or calling out of answers. You select the student you want to respond.
- Choral responses (everyone answering in unison) can be productive if the instructor is certain that everyone is participating. Such responses allow the instructor to move more quickly through some material and forces learners to use more than one of their senses (they have to hear **and** respond).
- Have students write the answers on notepads. Then circle around the room and read the answers to yourself so you can decide who should answer the question(s) out loud.
- Have students call on other students to provide responses.
- Have one learner summarize another's point.
- Play devil's advocate. Require students to defend their responses.
- Survey the class (thumbs up or down).
- Allow partner think time. (Students share thoughts with a partner and then the instructor opens the class for general discussion.)

RESPONDING TO STUDENT QUESTIONS AND RESPONSES

The most important aspect of questioning in the classroom is directed by the instructor. Nevertheless, the manner in which the instructor handles student questions and responses can affect the extent to which learning takes place. As learners ask questions, instructors should keep the following suggestions in mind:

- If you do not understand the question, ask the student to rephrase it or have another student rephrase the question.
- If a student asks an irrelevant or inappropriate question, do not waste class time. Encourage the participation, but tell the student where to find the answer or defer your response until after class.
- If you do not know the correct answer to a question, do not fabricate one. Simply tell the student that you will do some research and get back to the class with the correct response. Or ask if anyone in the class would like to respond. If another student does respond, be certain of the accuracy of the response.
- If a student's question relates to the lesson and is one you intended to ask of the class, do not simply give the response. Instead, ask another student to respond to the question.
- If a student asks a question that directly challenges your authority, remain calm but firm. Deal with the situation

after class. A confrontation in front of the entire class undermines your credibility. Professionals must remain above such behavior.

PERFORMANCE ACTIVITIES

1. For each of the lesson plans you prepared in Performance Activity 1, Section 1, of this chapter, prepare six key questions to ask the class. Each question should deal with a different level of thinking skills. Label each question based upon Bloom's taxonomy.
2. For each of the questions in Performance Activity 1 (above), prepare a follow-up question that requires a level of thinking different from that in the initial question.
3. For each performance outcome statement you wrote for Performance Activity 2 at the end of Chapter 2, write a question that corresponds with or measures the performance verb in each outcome statement.

SECTION III:
EVALUATION OF LEARNER PROGRESS

WHY EVALUATE?

Evaluation of learner progress has many purposes. The type of evaluation chosen by the instructor will depend upon the situation. Evaluation for program placement may be very different from evaluation for the diagnosis of learning difficulties. Evaluation simply for checking student understanding would probably be different from evaluation for reporting to parents or regulatory bodies. Evaluation for identifying difficulties in the design of the instructional program may be different yet. The point is that evaluation serves many purposes, and the method of evaluation selected must serve the purpose for which it is intended.

Generally, there are two overriding reasons for evaluating learner progress: to determine if the learners have achieved the expected outcomes of the lesson and, if not, to determine what needs to be taught to achieve the outcomes. The information collected in such evaluation benefits learners, instructors, and decision makers, for it indicates the knowledge, attitudes, and skills effected by the treatment. Frequent evaluation allows teachers the opportunity to adjust instruction as needed to better achieve the performance outcomes. In short, proper evaluation guides the actions of effective instructors.

WHAT IS EVALUATION?

Evaluation occurs when the instructor compares actual results with intended results. Often teacher judgment is a part of this equation, but truly effective evaluation removes as much judgment as possible.

Some argue that there is a difference between evaluation and assessment; they say assessment is merely the collection of data and evaluation is the actual use of the data or the judgment made based on the data. Although there may be some usefulness to this distinction, we will use the terms interchangeably. Gathering but not using data seems to be a fruitless exercise even though it does occur (for example, an instructor does not change instruction in spite of considerable student failure). Common usage has blurred whatever differences may exist between evaluation and assessment.

WHEN IS EVALUATION DONE?

At what point in a typical lesson does evaluation take place? Actually, it occurs at three different times. Prior to instruction there is preassessment, which allows instructors either to make good planning decisions or to diagnose present knowledge, attitudes, or skills. Preassessment focuses on determining what students already know. During instruction, ongoing assessment of learner progress occurs. Such evaluation allows the instructor to monitor and adjust instruction as necessary. After the instruction comes postassessment. This type of evaluation is useful for assigning student grades, providing data for the redesign of instruction, or confirming the degree of student learning.

INFORMAL EVALUATION

In a typical classroom considerable informal evaluation occurs on a daily basis. Such assessment may take the form of instructor observation, conversations with students, or independent assistance to learners in need. The most common type of informal assessment occurs through oral questioning. Effective questioning provides excellent information upon which instructors can adjust their lessons. Informal evaluation, however, is often not as useful as formal assessment. Formal assessment provides more valid data about which instructors are able to make informed decisions and judgments concerning the impact of the lesson.

FORMAL EVALUATION

Formal evaluation, as the name implies, is usually much more structured and methodical than informal evaluation. It consists of either a written or a performance-based exam or both.

Written Tests

The most common type of formal evaluation at all levels of education is still the written test. Written tests can be norm-referenced or criterion-referenced. Norm-referenced tests are typically standardized achievement or aptitude instruments. The intent of a norm-referenced test is to compare the performance of a specific group of students. This type of test is excellent at identifying the relative ability of members of a group compared with other members of the same group. Hence, a norm-referenced test could be helpful in any type of selection or sorting process. It is also helpful in reporting to regulatory bodies the relative achievement level of an identified group of students. Norm-referenced tests do not, however, clearly show the degree of mastery of performance outcomes resulting from instruction.

Criterion-referenced tests, on the other hand, measure learner performance against established criteria. For that reason, criterion-referenced instruments are more helpful in measuring student progress and adjusting classroom instruction.

Preparing Written Tests

In preparing written tests, instructors should be aware of the strengths and weaknesses of various types of test items. For example, remember that simple recall questions do little to extend or measure learning. Instructors should make certain that they select test items that show the degree to which performance outcomes have been met. The test items should directly match the difficulty of the objective. Beyond performance outcomes, there may be other objectives that require some type of measurement. Once again, the instructor must carefully construct test items that measure those objectives as well.

Test items usually fall into two categories: objective and subjective. Objective items are typically true/false, multiple choice, and matching. Grading of objective test items requires little judgment on the part of the instructor. Subjective items are either short answer (completion, definition, and identification) or essay. Grading of subjective test items requires considerable judgment on the part of the instructor. Each of these different types of test items have advantages and disadvantages.

Objective Test Items

True/False. True/false items require the student to identify the accuracy of terms, definitions, and so on. By using these items, the instructor is able to sample a great deal of material. Accordingly, true/false items are an efficient use of time. They are also relatively easy to construct. Unfortunately, true/false items are often only used to measure lower levels of thinking processes, and there is a significant guessing variable, which limits their usefulness. Some also claim that exposing students to a number of wrong answers can be harmful. If the instructor chooses to use true/false questions, he or she should do so with considerable caution.

Multiple Choice. Multiple choice items are among the most versatile, because they can measure higher order thinking skills. Such items will be either an incomplete sentence or a direct question. The most obvious advantage of multiple choice questions is ease of grading. The probability of guessing correctly diminishes if the instructor selects the items carefully. Additionally, item analysis of incorrect responses allows for adjustments in teaching to meet identified needs. The biggest difficulty for the instructor in writing multiple choice questions is designing plausible alternatives. Multiple choice questions suffer from the same weakness as all objective questions: they do not require learners to express themselves in their own words.

Matching. Matching is actually a form of multiple choice; the only difference is that in matching there are multiple items as well as multiple alternatives. A major strength of matching is the ability to measure a great deal of material in a short period. Also, items are easily constructed. Unfortunately, matching items are used too often for simple recall. Instructors must be careful to give clear directions, keep the number of items small, and arrange the lists in some type of logical order. Three-column matching is another possibility. For example, the second column may simply identify the cause of a problem mentioned in the first column. The third column, however, may extend the second column by requiring the selection of a solution to the cause identified in the second column. Now the instructor is able to measure beyond the recall and comprehension levels of thinking skills.

Subjective Test Items

Subjective items require judgment on the part of the instructor who must determine the acceptability of the response. Objective items, on the other hand, are much less open to interpretation.

Short Answer: Completion, Definition, and Identification. Short-answer-type items are excellent ways to measure knowledge of facts, principles, and processes. If written properly, they are natural for students, and they can assess higher-order thinking skills. These types of items require concise answers, often single words or phrases. The instructor should put the blank at the end of the sentence and should not simply pull sentences from the text. The biggest problem faced by instructors is the difficulty in being objective if a response is almost, but not exactly, correct. In short answer items, instructors also have to deal with the problem of inappropriate grammar.

Essay. The essay has the ability to require students to use all levels of the thinking processes. By emphasizing expression rather than mere recall, the essay is able to demonstrate complex behaviors and the improvement of writing skills. The nature of the essay may require a limited response from the student, or it may force the student to use higher-order thinking skills. Instructors who use essays should make certain that the essays reflect the major emphases of the course, come with specific directions, and indicate a preferred time limit. Before grading student papers, the instructor should prepare a model answer. The biggest disadvantages of the essay are the considerable testing and grading time, the inability to survey a broad body of content, and the relative lack of reliability in scoring.

Performance Tests

Written tests are not always the best choice for evaluating technique. In many cases it is preferable to have the students demonstrate performance. Performance tests measure how well the student can perform a particular process or create a product. Instructors can use performance tests during all phases of instruction. These types of tests usually require the learner to do something (complete a task or product). That requirement should relate directly to the performance outcome (for example, the student must develop a marketing plan or perform some algebraic operations under certain conditions). Instructors must clearly state the standards by which the they will judge performance. Additionally, the rating scale chosen by the instructor must relate to the performance outcome and the stated criteria. If the student does not complete the process or product in an acceptable manner, he or she must practice that performance until mastery occurs.

LEARNING DOMAINS

Bloom's *Taxonomy of Educational Objectives* deals with only one of the three areas of learning, the cognitive domain. In evaluation, instructors frequently deal with the other two domains: the affective (attitudes) and the psychomotor (skills). Some authors suggest a different classification for learning domains, but we will use these three for the sake of simplicity.

The affective domain creates additional, unusual problems in relation to evaluation. It is extremely difficult to determine actual attitudes. While you can infer whether a student has a particular attitude based on his or her performance, it is exceedingly more difficult to determine if he or she actually has that attitude. Regardless of the difficulty, however, there is reason for attempting to measure attitudes. Such measurement may not be as precise as the measurement of knowledge and skills, but it may be equally important in the overall plan of the instructor. Certainly there is value in teaching some things that are not precisely measurable as long as teaching nonmeasurable or poorly measurable content is not all you teach.

The psychomotor domain deals with the measurement of motor, physical, and manipulative skills. Vocational classes lend themselves quite nicely to this type of evaluation. Most psychomotor skills require new cognitive skills as well. In fact, the distinction between psychomotor and cognitive skills is becoming blurred. Most **job skills** require new learning in both domains.

SUGGESTIONS FOR EVALUATION

A variety of evaluation decisions confront instructors on a daily basis. Remember the following suggestions when you are making decisions.

- Evaluate often. Much of the evaluation can be informal, but the instructor needs formalized information in order to make adjustments and provide feedback to students.
- Provide a wide variety of evaluation techniques over the duration of a course. Variety allows students with different learning styles to demonstrate learning.
- Provide multiple weekly grades of some type for all students. Multiple grades can be motivational and may increase attendance. In addition, it is unfair to students to give only a mid-term and a final exam. An instructor who does this simply does not care about evaluation of student progress or instructional design.
- Adjust your teaching based upon evaluation results.
- Choose your method of assigning grades carefully. If you decide to grade on a curve, understand that such a practice assumes that your class represents a normal distribution of ability. In fact, few classes have such a distribution; hence, the curve will be unfair for many students. Likewise, the ten-point scale has limitations. Use of a scale assumes that the instructor has written the perfect test and all the students have to do is perform. Few tests written by instructors are perfect (both valid and reliable). For these reasons, tests that require students to achieve a specific criterion are often the best alternative for measuring student progress in the classroom and adjusting instruction.
- If you plan to award grades for effort, do not mix those grades with achievement grades.
- Understand that both positive and negative results on tests reflect upon the instructor. Do not accept credit for students doing well unless you are also willing to accept blame for students doing poorly.
- Make sure the evaluation technique you select is appropriate for the performance outcome of the lesson.
- Provide students with the criteria for receiving their final grade at the beginning of the course.
- Grade tests quickly, return them to students in a timely manner, and review the results with the learners.

PERFORMANCE ACTIVITIES

1. In Performance Activity 4 of Chapter 2, you were asked to prepare three performance outcomes for each course you teach. For each of those outcomes, describe the evaluation techniques you will use or did use (for example, type of test, type of questions). Why did you choose those techniques?
2. For each evaluation technique you chose in Performance Activity 1 (above), provide an alternate way you could measure the same outcome.
3. Review the evaluation techniques described by a colleague in response to Performance Activity 1 (above). Prepare a written critique of those techniques. Share your critique with your colleague.

PART II
OBSERVATION OF LIVE INSTRUCTION

The teacher's problem is to protect the spirit of inquiry, to keep it from becoming blasé from over excitement, wooden from routine, fossilized through dogmatic instruction, or dissipated by random exercise upon trivial things.

John Dewey

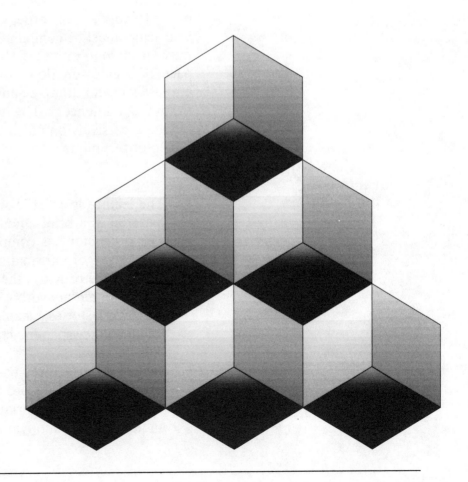

To complete this part of the workbook, have the accompanying video readily available. The performance activities in Chapter 5 relate directly to various portions of the video as well as to the following discussion of four different modes of instruction.

As we saw in Chapter 3, there are a wide variety of modes of instruction from which instructors may choose. Seldom does one mode achieve the desired results. Most often a combination of instructional modes results in an effective lesson. Hence, selecting the appropriate mode(s) is an important aspect of the planning process. Equally important is understanding **why** to choose a specific mode. In making a choice, the instructor should consider the content of the lesson, learning styles of the students, his or her own teaching style, available resources, and the performance outcome of the lesson.

Four of the more commonly used modes of instruction are the lecture, small group activity, demonstration, and laboratory. Each of these modes of instruction has advantages and disadvantages.

LECTURE

The lecture is among the most widely used, and abused, modes of instruction. In order to deliver a lecture effectively, instructors must be completely familiar with the material. They must speak loudly and clearly, and they must be careful that the pace of the lesson flows smoothly. An effective lecturer is enthusiastic and dramatic and watches for nonverbal responses from the audience. The lecturer must be natural without relying excessively on notes. Moving around the room is often a helpful technique to use while delivering the lecture.

Advantages of the Lecture

▶ The lecture is an efficient way to deliver a broad range of material in a brief amount of time.
▶ The instructor has complete control over the content and sequencing of information.
▶ The lecture provides the opportunity to use a wide variety of supplementary verbal illustrations (analogies, anecdotes, humorous stories, examples, and so on) and visual aids (pictures, newspapers, charts, video, and so on) to assist in making a point.
▶ An effective lecturer has a unique opportunity to get the attention of and inspire an audience.
▶ The lecture is appropriate for any age group as long as the audience is self-motivated.

▸ The lecture is an excellent way to demonstrate deductive reasoning (teaching from known facts to a logical conclusion), provide direct instruction, and develop concepts.

Disadvantages of the Lecture

▸ The lecture is a large group activity, whereas most learning takes place individually.

▸ The lecture is essentially one-way communication, unless it is combined with another mode of instruction. As such, there is no significant opportunity for the instructor to check for understanding. The most effective method is to combine oral questioning and lecturing to achieve two-way communication.

▸ The lecture does not allow active involvement of students. Long spans of passivity are detrimental to learning.

▸ In lectures there is a heavy reliance on self-instruction since the instructor merely presents the material. Although the instructor may encourage student practice, any significant guided or independent practice that demonstrates mastery of the concept or material occurs on the student's own time.

▸ Transfer of learning relies totally upon the instructor. The instructor may remind students about how information transfers, but students are not actively involved in this thought process.

▸ Other than for short segments, the lecture is largely inappropriate for skill-type lessons.

SMALL GROUPS

Using small groups in a classroom setting is a second mode of instruction frequently used by skilled instructors. This mode of instruction can be extremely effective if implemented appropriately.

Typically, the instructor selects a topic for group discussion. The instructor then orients the students to the topic, provides time limitations, gives guidelines for the activity, and allows the groups to go to work. While the groups are discussing the topic or problem, the instructor circulates through the room to keep groups on task, encourage interaction, ask leading questions, clarify problems, and assess the degree to which the performance outcome is being met. After reaching consensus, the groups may report to the entire class. The instructor may then summarize the results and plan the next steps. The class may choose to discuss the group process itself.

Advantages of Small Groups

▸ Small groups are versatile: they can be used for a variety of topics and material.

- Small groups can be effective in solving problems and handling controversial issues.
- Small groups require active participation.
- Small groups can be especially helpful in dealing with the affective domain (feelings, attitudes, values, and so on).
- Small groups help develop interpersonal and leadership skills.
- Small group activities stimulate critical thinking skills.
- Small groups allow students to become involved in the transfer of learning.
- Small groups provide excellent opportunities for using inductive reasoning (general validity is inferred from observed validity in particular cases) or the inquiry method (teaching through questioning).

Disadvantages of Small Groups

- Groups can be sidetracked easily.
- Groups are usually unable to deal with a breadth of material. (Cooperative learning groups are different; refer to the next section titled A Special Note on Groups.)
- Groups are easily dominated by a few students, thus eliminating the benefit of active participation on the part of all students.
- Group activity is time-consuming.
- Some questions may be left unanswered.
- Group consensus may reflect only opinions if proper preparation did not occur.
- Placing students in groups properly can be difficult.

A Special Note on Groups

The concept of group activity takes on an entirely new meaning when viewed in the context of cooperative learning. Johnson, Johnson, and Holubec (1986) suggest that cooperative learning is not only effective but necessary for growth and competitiveness in our country. They believe that the ability to work in groups may, in fact, be the most important skill learned in school.

In some ways cooperative learning is similar to traditional group activity. There are, however, significant differences. According to Johnson, Johnson, and Holubec (1986, p. 59), there are several basic elements of a cooperatively structured learning activity:

- Positive interdependence: In contrast to traditional groups, cooperative learning groups depend upon each other in a variety of ways. For example, each member of the group may be responsible for a certain portion of the material. That person must learn the material and then teach it to other members of the group. Group members may also depend upon each other for their grades, since the performance of each member of the group affects each individual's grade. Essentially, the members of the group must develop an attitude of sink or swim together.

▶ Individual accountability: As opposed to typical group activity found in many classrooms, cooperative learning emphasizes the individual responsibility of each student to learn the material and be held accountable for it. Although working cooperatively enhances the likelihood of learning the material, each student must be able to demonstrate mastery of the subject material.

▶ Face-to-face-interaction: Students summarize and elaborate orally on the material being learned.

▶ Appropriate use of collaborative skills: Students are taught social skills and how to function in groups.

▶ Processing: Students are given the opportunity to discuss the group process itself and how well the group is functioning.

Johnson, Johnson, and Holubec provide considerable research to support their beliefs about cooperative learning. Consult the bibliography if you wish to pursue this concept.

DEMONSTRATION

Demonstration is the third frequently used mode of instruction. An effective demonstration requires careful planning; it must flow in a logical order with key points emphasized throughout. The demonstration is an appropriate technique for showing students how to perform a task or for explaining a concept. The keys to a good demonstration are the questioning that takes place and the opportunity students have to practice the modeled behavior.

Advantages of Demonstration

▶ Demonstrations are appropriate for explaining a concept or showing how to perform a task.

▶ The demonstration is an effective method for getting students to think at the application level of thinking skills.

▶ Demonstrations can be thought-provoking, particularly if done in a discovery fashion. (Students discover the outcome of the lesson by observing the results of the demonstration or by practicing the demonstration itself.)

▶ The demonstration allows active participation. Practicing the demonstration, role-playing, negotiating, and interviewing are especially effective techniques for engaging students in the lesson.

- Demonstrations provide an opportunity for excellent transfer of learning if effective questioning accompanies them.
- The instructor is able to adjust the pace of the lesson as necessary.

Disadvantages of Demonstration

- The time and expense involved in preparing and giving the demonstration are often significant. The instructor must decide if a demonstration is the most efficient use of time.
- Materials and equipment are often in limited supply (especially for subsequent student practice).
- The size of the group may be a limitation. Students must be able to see and hear the demonstration.
- Unless the instructor combines the demonstration with effective questioning and student practice, there is no opportunity to check for understanding.
- Demonstrations require extensive planning and organization so that crucial steps are not skipped.

THE LABORATORY

A fourth mode of instruction used frequently in discovery or skill-type classes is the laboratory. An effective laboratory class is usually preceded by some other mode of instruction, for example, lecture or demonstration. Following this introduction, the teacher provides written instructions to the students; then the students perform in the lab. Throughout the lab, the instructor moves around the room to the various individuals or groups and provides assistance, asks and answers questions, and gives feedback. Provision of appropriate materials is a key to a successful lab.

Advantages of the Laboratory

- Students are actively involved and learn by doing.
- The laboratory can be individualized to the interests and abilities of each student.
- Laboratories can be thought-provoking and allow students to engage in discovery activities.
- Instructors are able to assess student understanding as they circulate through the room.
- Instructors have the opportunity to encourage students to transfer learning in the lab to previously learned material.

Disadvantages of the Laboratory

- Frequently, equipment and supplies are unavailable or insufficient.
- The breadth of material that can be covered is limited.
- The time involved in planning and delivering a lab can be considerable. Instructors have to weigh the efficiency of

the lab approach against the performance outcome and other possible modes of instruction.

- ► The lab requires self-directed students who are capable of handling the freedom inherent in a lab setting.
- ► The pace of the lesson is difficult to control.
- ► A lab can be extremely disorganized if instructions are unclear.

CHAPTER 5

PERFORMANCE ACTIVITIES FOR THE VIDEO CLIPS

A great teacher is like a great artist. It may even be the greatest of arts since the medium is the human mind and spirit....To a large extent, the student is the unsigned manuscript of the teacher. What deathless power lies in the hands of such a person.

John Ernst Steinbeck

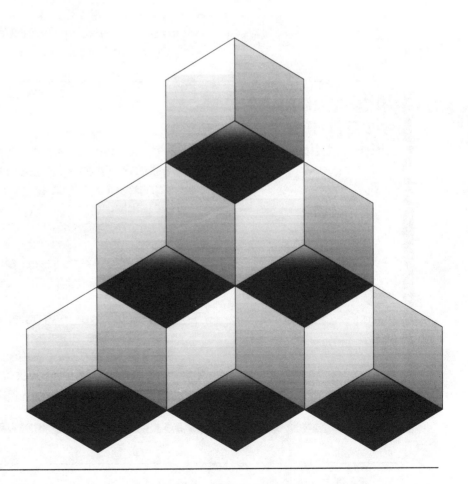

Part I of this workbook provided a great deal of background material. Now you have the opportunity to put the pieces of the puzzle together by evaluating video clips of live instruction.

First we must recognize the inherent difficulties in the video-workbook format. Because of the brevity of the clips, it is virtually impossible to determine exactly what the teacher attempted to do. It is also difficult to determine what transpired before the lessons, what the teacher did after the clip, and what the teacher intends to do in the future. Additionally, the video editing process may have deleted information you need to make a completely informed decision about the questions that follow. These decisions were intentional; lessons were altered to permit teacher evaluations.

Despite these difficulties, we can learn a great deal from watching someone else teach. After watching the video clips and completing the performance activities that follow, observe a colleague teach in your own institution. And if you really want a unique experience, videotape one of your own lessons and see what you think!

As you watch the lessons, remember to use the Classroom Observation Form found in the companion *Instructional Leadership* workbook.

Now view video clip 1 on Part II of the accompanying videotape: Analyzing Your Fog Index. You will be directed back to the following performance activities after the lesson.

PERFORMANCE ACTIVITIES
Video Clip 1

1. Did the instructor state a performance outcome for this lesson? Was it measurable? Was it important and significant? What are your suggestions for improving the statement of performance outcomes?
2. What modes of instruction were used? Were they appropriate? Describe why or why not.
3. Were visual aids used effectively? How?
4. Describe the guided practice that took place during the lesson.
5. How did the instructor monitor student progress? Describe the questioning techniques used. How did the instructor keep students involved?
6. Was the material covered in this lesson transferred in any way to previously learned material?

Now view video clip 2: Using a Dictation Machine. You will be directed back to the following performance activities after the lesson.

PERFORMANCE ACTIVITIES
Video Clip 2

1. Was the performance outcome stated clearly? Describe how you might improve it.
2. What modes of instruction were used? Were they appropriate?
3. Were students actively involved in the lesson? Describe the independent practice that took place.
4. Did the instructor attempt to make the lesson interesting for students? Did he show enthusiasm for the subject matter? How?
5. How did the instructor monitor student performance?
6. Was there a review at the end of the lesson?

Now view video clip 3: The Apparel Arts Lesson. You will be directed back to the following performance activities after the lesson.

PERFORMANCE ACTIVITIES
Video Clip 3

1. Was the performance outcome stated clearly?
2. What modes of instruction were used? Were they appropriate?
3. Were all students able to see the demonstration? What changes would you recommend in this portion of the lesson?
4. Describe the teacher's questioning technique. How did the teacher monitor student progress?
5. Describe the atmosphere in the classroom.

Now view video clip 4: Time Management and Planning. You will be directed back to the following performance activities after the lesson.

PERFORMANCE ACTIVITIES
Video Clip 4

1. How did the teacher relate this lesson and its intended outcomes to previously learned material? Were the outcomes clear?
2. What modes of instruction were used? Were they appropriate? Were they effective?
3. Did the groups appear to have a clear understanding of the task? Did they function effectively? Describe the group dynamics and degree of active involvement.
4. How did the instructor assist and focus the groups?
5. How did the instructor use reinforcement?
6. Describe the instructor's review of the lesson.

Now view video clip 5: Psychology/Self-Assessment — Barriers to Education. You will be directed back to the following performance activities after the lesson.

PERFORMANCE ACTIVITIES
Video Clip 5

1. Were the performance outcomes stated clearly? What components, if any, of a good performance outcome statement were missing?
2. What modes of instruction were used? Were they appropriate? Is this an example of cooperative learning?
3. Were students interested and actively involved?
4. Was there any transfer to previous learning? If so, describe.

Now view video clip 6: Electronics Lab. You will be directed back to the following performance activities after the lesson.

PERFORMANCE ACTIVITIES
Video Clip 6

1. Were the performance outcomes stated clearly? Were they measurable? What components, if any, of a good statement of performance outcomes were missing?
2. What modes of instruction were used? Were they appropriate and effective?
3. Describe the guided and independent practice that occurred. Did the teacher adjust his instruction?
4. Were instructions for the lab activity clear to you? If not, what would you have done to make certain the instructions were clear?
5. How did the instructor monitor student progress?
6. Did students appear to grasp the material? Will some type of reteaching be necessary?

Now view video clip 7: Office Automation — Optical Disc Technology. You will be directed back to the following performance activities after the lesson.

PERFORMANCE ACTIVITIES
Video Clip 7

1. Were the performance outcomes stated clearly? If not, what components were missing?
2. What modes of instruction were used? Were they appropriate? What kind of planning was required for this lesson? Was this a review lesson or information taught for the first time?
3. How did the instructor monitor student progress?
4. Describe the effectiveness of the instructor's questioning technique. Was there two-way communication?
5. Did the instructor reinforce student responses? How?

Now view video clip 8: Databases and Information Management. You will be directed back to the following performance activities after the lesson.

PERFORMANCE ACTIVITIES
Video Clip 8

1. Were the performance outcomes clear to you? If not, what components were missing?
2. What modes of instruction were used? Were they effective?
3. How did the instructor apply the lesson to a real-life situation?
4. Describe the independent practice that took place.
5. Describe how the instructor made effective use of feedback to students. Did she use the question-answer-question format of oral questioning? Did you see the instructor monitor and adjust her instruction?

BIBLIOGRAPHY

BIBLIOGRAPHY

(Publications or papers sponsored by NIE can now be obtained from the Office of Educational Research and Improvement, Washington, D.C.)

Barnes, Carol P. "Questioning in College Classrooms." In *Studies of College Teaching*, edited by Carolyn L. Ellner and Carol Barnes. Lexington: Lexington Books, 1983.

Bloom, Benjamin, et al. *The Taxonomy of Educational Objectives. Handbook I: The Cognitive Domain.* New York: David McKay, 1956.

Brookover, Walter B., and Lezotte, Lawrence W. *Changes in School Characteristics Coincident with Changes in Student Achievement.* East Lansing: Michigan State University, College of Urban Development, 1977.

"Conduct Group Discussions, Panel Discussions, and Symposiums, Module C-2," American Association for Vocational Instructional Materials. Athens: The University of Georgia, 1977.

Davies, Ivor Kevin. *Instructional Technique.* New York: McGraw-Hill, 1981.

"Demonstrate a Concept or Principle, Module C-17," American Association for Vocational Instructional Materials. Athens: The University of Georgia, 1987.

"Demonstrate a Manipulative Skill, Module C-16," American Association for Vocational Instructional Materials. Athens: The University of Georgia, 1987.

"Direct Student Laboratory Experience, Module C-7," American Association for Vocational Instructional Materials. Athens: The University of Georgia, 1987.

Edmonds, Ronald. "A Discussion of the Literature and Issues Related to Effective Schooling," vol. 6. St. Louis: CEMREL, Inc., 1979.

Edmonds, Ronald. "Programs of School Improvement: An Overview." National Institute of Education Conference, February 1982.

Emmer, Edmund T., and Evertson, Carolyn M. *Effective Management at the Beginning of the School Year in Junior High Classes.* University of Texas at Austin, R&D Report No. 6107, March 1980.

"Employ Reinforcement Techniques, Module C-13," American Association for Vocational Instructional Materials. Athens: The University of Georgia, 1986.

Erickson, Richard C., and Wentling, Tim L. *Measuring Student Growth*. Urbana, Ill.: Griffon Press, 1976.

Gagne, Robert M., and Briggs, Leslie J. *Principles of Instructional Design*. New York: Holt, Rinehart, and Winston, 1979.

Goddard, M. Lee. "Excellence in Teaching — Attainable Goal or Unrealistic Expectation?" *The Ohio Business Teacher* (April 1988): 30-37.

Goslin, David A. Teachers and Testing. New York: Russell Sage Foundation, 1967.

Harris, John., Hillenmeyer, Susan., and Foran, James V. *Quality Assurance for Private Career Schools*. Washington, D.C., Association of Independent Colleges and Schools, 1989.

Hunter, Madeline. "Beyond Rereading Dewey . . . What's Next? A Response to Gibboney." Educational Leadership, February (1987): 51-53.

Hunter, Madeline. "Knowing, Teaching, and Supervising." In *Using What We Know About Teaching*. Edited by Philip Hosford, 169-192. Alexandria, Va.: ASCD, 1984.

Hunter, Madeline. *Motivation Theory for Teachers*. El Segundo, Calif.: TIP Publications, 1980.

Hunter, Madeline. *Reinforcement Theory for Teachers*. El Segundo, Calif.: TIP Publications, 1980.

Hunter, Madeline. *Retention Theory for Teachers*. El Segundo, Calif.: TIP Publications, 1980.

Hunter, Madeline. *Teach for Transfer*. El Segundo, Calif.: TIP Publications, 1980.

Hunter, Madeline. "Teaching is Decision Making." *Educational Leadership* (October 1979): 62-67.

Hunter, Madeline. *Teach More Faster*. El Segundo, Calif.: TIP Publications, 1980.

Hunter, Madeline. "What's Wrong with Madeline Hunter?" Educational Leadership (February 1985): 57-60.

Hyslop, David. "Instructional Traits of Effective Teachers." *The Ohio Business Teacher* (April 1988): 16-21.

"Introduce a Lesson, Module C-10," American Association for Vocational Instructional Materials. Athens: The University of Georgia, 1983.

Johnson, David W., Johnson, Roger T., and Holubec, Edyth J. *Circles of Learning: Cooperation in the Classroom*. Edina, Mo.: Interaction Book Company, 1986.

Johnson, David W., Johnson, Roger T., and Holubec, Edyth J. *Structuring Cooperative Learning: Lesson Plans for Teachers*. Edina, Mo.: Interaction Book Company, 1987.

Johnson, Kerry A. "The Foundations of Instructional Design." In *Instructional Design, New Alternatives for Effective Education and Training*, edited by Kerry A. Johnson and Lin J. Foa, 3-15. Washington, D.C.: American Council on Education and Macmillan, 1989.

"Manage the Adult Instructional Process, Module N-5," American Association for Vocational Instructional Materials. Athens: The University of Georgia, 1986.

Miles, Matthew B., Farrar, Eleanor, and Neufeld, Barbara. "The Extent of Adoption of Effective Schools Programs." Paper prepared for the National Commission on Excellence in Education, Washington, D.C. January 1983.

"Plan Instruction for Adults, Module N-4," American Association for Vocational Instructional Materials. Athens: The University of Georgia, 1987.

"Prepare to Work with Adult Learners, Module N-1," American Association for Vocational Instructional Materials. Athens: The University of Georgia, 1987.

Popham, W. James. *An Evaluation Guidebook*. Los Angeles: The Instructional Objectives Exchange, 1972.

"Present an Illustrated Talk, Module C-15," American Association for Vocational Instructional Materials. Athens: The University of Georgia, 1989.

Rosenshine, Barak. "Teaching Functions in an Instructional Program." Paper prepared for National Institute of Education, February 1982.

Scannell, Dale P., and Tracy, Dick. *Testing and Measurement in the Classroom*. Boston: Houghton Mifflin, 1975.

"Summarize a Lesson, Module C-11," American Association for Vocational Instructional Materials. Athens: The University of Georgia, 1983.

Troisi, Nicholas F. *Effective Teaching and Student Achievement*. Reston, Va.: NASSP, 1983.

Troyer, Donald L. "Formulating Performance Objectives." In *Developing Teacher Competencies*, edited by James E. Weigand, 44-80. Englewood Cliffs: Prentice-Hall, 1971.

Van Patten, James. "What is Instructional Design?" In *Instructional Design, New Alternatives for Effective Education and Training*, edited by Kerry A. Johnson and Lin J. Foa, 16-31. Washington, D.C.: American Council on Education and Macmillan, 1989.

Wiggins, Grant. "The Futility of Trying to Teach Everything of Importance," *Educational Leadership* (November 1989).

Wolfe, Patricia, and Robbins, Pam. *Instructional Decisions for Long Term Learning*. Alexandria, Va.: ASCD, 1987.

A FINAL THOUGHT

Those who can, do. Those who can't, teach.
Misinformed Anonymous Cynic

Like many other institutions in American society, the teaching profession has undergone increased scrutiny in recent years. Some of the criticism it has received is well deserved.

Virtually every American has experienced the educational system. As a result, self-anointed experts on the ills of schooling abound. Additionally, ivory tower theorists, who do not have to implement what they preach, peddle instant solutions to the problems teachers face.

Teachers are not the problem. Indeed, they are the solution to the problem. Certainly teachers need to work at regaining the respect of those they serve. Even the harshest critics, however, must recognize that teaching is not what it used to be. Because policymakers or administrators are unwilling to commit sufficient resources to the operation of an institution, teachers become quasi-administrators. Because managers are unwilling to provide the time necessary for continuous professional growth, teachers simply indulge in standard recipes for improvement.

This workbook and accompanying video are not intended to be another such recipe. Teaching is too complex and laden with decisions to reduce it to a quick fix. Yes, we have attempted to simplify and demystify what teachers do on a regular basis. We hope to have provided subject matter experts with some basic tools for success in the classroom. Nothing, however, will replace a genuine love of helping students, a commitment to sustained study, and years of experience. Only then can one truly become a master teacher.